AF428605

What Made You Smile Today?

Prologue

The objective of this book is to provide questions to offer an open, meaningful, and foundation building dialogue
with the children in your life. The younger the better, however, I encourage you to start at any age.
The idea is based on a simple practice I began with my children when they were very young.

A child begins to be socially active before they can verbalize and share their experiences.
Many parents, grandparents, and guardians encounter the feelings of separation for the first time when
children begin daycare, preschool, or kindergarten. Asking the simple, "How was your day?", seemed vague to me.
I wanted to know what my children experienced during their day, the events I missed, and the emotions and feelings
that accompanied their experiences.

To begin this practice, carve out some quiet time for both of you. Bedtime worked best for my family.
Put aside your devices to allow for undivided attention.
Your children will look forward to sharing their day with you and it will develop into a treasured tradition.
I found that the practice of asking important questions led to a relationship built on love, trust, and genuine interest.
A foundation, that to this day, gives the adult children in my life the capacity to share openly and honestly,
knowing we can walk through this life together.

Use the questions in this book as guideposts.
Soon you will start your own personal dialogue custom-made for your individual circumstances.
Be a good listener.
Be present, hold space, and help the children in your life feel supported, valued, and understood.

I lovingly dedicate this book to
Eleanor Catherine

What made you smile today?

How was your day today?
What made it a good day?

Did anything bad happen today?

Would you like to talk about it?

What made you laugh today?

Did you make someone laugh?

Who said or did something funny?

Did you know that laughing is good for you?

Laughing is healthy because it produces positive energy inside and outside of you!

ZOO
What made you smile today?
Did you see an animal or hear a song
that made you smile?

Your smile
is one of the most beautiful features on your face!

Did anything make you sad today?
What happened?
Did you cry?

Every person experiences sad moments.
It is ok to feel sad and it is ok to cry.

Sometimes we don't know what to say
so our tears speak for us.
Can you think of anything that could have
changed so you don't feel sad?

Did you see something new on your walk or ride to school today?
SCHOOL

Perhaps you saw something
new that you didn't notice yesterday.

Look for something new tomorrow
so we can talk about it.

Were you kind today
or did you see someone else being kind?

How were you kind today?

Was there an event that could have been handled differently if kindness was practiced today?

What are you grateful for today?

**Count five things that you are grateful for today
You may use these or think of your own**

1) I am grateful to be me.

2) I am grateful for the people who love me.

3) I am grateful for the people I love.

4) I am grateful for my pets

5) I am grateful for my heartbeat

Practicing gratitude allows positive energy to flow from your heart and connects you to others.

Did you share an object, a thought, a story, or a smile today?

Would you like to tell me about it?

Sharing
is an example of your heart speaking.

Do you have anymore thoughts that you would like to share?

I am grateful that we have this time together.

And

I am grateful that I have you to share it with!

A kiss goodnight and one more question before you fall asleep ...

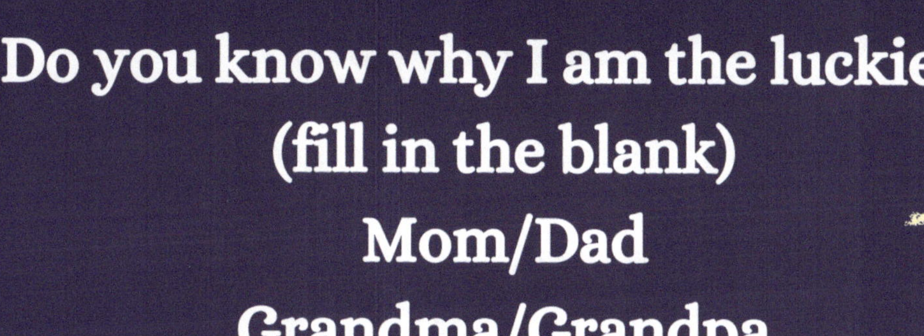

Do you know why I am the luckiest
(fill in the blank)
Mom/Dad
Grandma/Grandpa
in the whole world?

Because I received the best gift and
that gift is
YOU!

Acknowledgments

I want to thank my sons, Nick and Derrick, for choosing me to be their mom
and trusting me with their hearts.
Thank you to my husband and life partner, Russell, for your love and
continued support in all of my endeavors.

Thank you to my friend, Angelina, for your unique talent and for
providing the illustrations for the characters in this book.

I am grateful for each and everyone of you.

Micki Abels is a wife, mother, and grandmother.
She is a writer, blogger, certified transformational life coach,
and a meditation instructor.
She loves yoga, reading, and spending time
with her family.

Angelina Lamie is an 8 -year-old aspiring artist
who loves gymnastics, yoga, and swimming.
She is an amazing little sister to three brothers and
an awesome aunt to one nephew.